Navigating a Narcissist

BY

Leanne Sumnall

THE EMPIRE
PUBLISHERS

131 Finsbury Pavement, London EC2A 1NT
https://www.theempirepublishers.co.uk/

Our books may be purchased in bulk for promotional,
educational, or business use.

Please contact The Empire Publishers at +44 20 4579 8116, or
by email at support@theempirepublishers.co.uk
First Edition

Dedication

To my amazing husband Jeremy and beautiful daughter Evangeline-mai – with both of your unwavering and constant support and love – I can be me. I love you both so very much.

To Pamela, Sandra, Maxine, and Wendy – who were and are the foundation and rocks in my career.

Zoe, Alison, Jenny, Kathryn, Sarah, Iesher and many more – thank you for your friendship over many years and having my back.

'Out of the kindness of others comes growth of self.' – LS

About the Author

Leanne Sumnall lives in Staffordshire with her family and is a Psychotherapeutic counsellor in private practice. Her modality is Psychodynamic, in which attachment and relationships have always been her passion in helping others navigate their individual unique journeys with others.

Through Leanne's educational journey, she realised her early attachment style and the impact it had on her own relationships. This realisation made her even more invested in helping others within the three different attachment styles – navigate safely to a secure attachment style.

After working with clients within an NHS Staff Support well-being service as well as an Addiction Recovery organisation in Staffordshire – it was always her goal to set up in private practice to work with clients with a wide and diverse range of presenting issues – but to specialise in relationships, attachment, and the impacts of narcissism.

Leanne works with clients face-to-face in Staffordshire, as well as online and by telephone UK-wide. She has a very client-centric approach to her talking therapy and is passionate about providing a safe, confidential space for her clients to build a trusting working relationship to work towards a brighter sense of self and future with validation, empathy, acceptance, and no judgment.

At the time of printing, Leanne is a registered member of the BACP (British Association for Counselling and Psychotherapy), a Police Firearm Officer Association (PFOA) approved counsellor, a practitioner for Tonic

Wellbeing (promoting health and well-being in the workplace), an affiliate of SP Bespoke Wellbeing (a private addiction recovery organisation) and a host - online and in-person - of EMPOWER networking for Counsellors, Therapists, Coaches, and students. EMPOWER was a niche that needed filling for Leanne, to allow peers a chance to gain support, friendships, and collaborations in their fields.

To find out more about Leanne and her associations and affiliations:

www.mazecounselling.com

www.choosetonic.co.uk

www.spbespoke.com

www.bacp.co.uk

www.pfoa.co.uk

EMPOWER – via Eventbrite or www.facebook.com/mazecounsellingservices

Contents

Foreword

It's with a warm heart and an open mind that I welcome you to 'Navigating a Narcissist'. As a psychotherapist, I've journeyed alongside many who've found themselves entwined in the complex dance of narcissistic relationships. It's a path that can be as bewildering as it is painful, yet, within it, there's a rich landscape for growth and understanding.

This book is a beacon of light for anyone navigating these cloudy waters. I have crafted a guide that's not just insightful but also incredibly approachable. I unravel the complexity of narcissistic dynamics, making sense of the various personalities, attachment styles, and love languages that play into these relationships.

But 'Navigating a Narcissist' goes beyond just understanding; it's about empowering you. It's about giving you the tools to build healthier boundaries, protect and reclaim your sense of self, and cultivate relationships that are nurturing and genuine.

Embarking on this journey, you're not just reading a book; you're stepping onto a path of discovery. You'll explore not only the nature of narcissism but also the resilience and strength that lies within you. This book celebrates personal growth, understanding, and the human spirit's capacity to transform challenge into opportunity.

I'm so excited for you to dive in. May you find clarity, hope, and a renewed sense of empowerment in these pages. Your journey toward healthier relationships and a stronger sense of self starts now.

With all my support,

Leanne Sumnall, MBACP

Psychotherapeutic Counsellor.

Introduction

Why I wrote this book?

I wanted to write a book, not only from a therapist's point of view – but with lived experience of an attachment to narcissists.

Narcissists leave more questions than answers, with nothing ever making sense. I wanted this book to highlight not only the experience and questions but when you read this, you find yourself nodding your head – and saying – 'yes that was/is me!'. Not all of this content will resonate with every reader, but it allows you to realise your life was and is real, that you are validated, and that there has never been anything wrong with you. It is always a reflection of the narcissist – not a reflection on you.

I wanted this to be an easy-to-read book that anyone can pick up and find answers or gain greater understanding – whether you are navigating your own journey or helping someone through or out of their experiences. It is not necessarily a self-help book – but a book to show you are not alone. You can choose the sections that you think are relevant to you or others – or read from cover to cover to give you a greater insight into narcissism and narcissistic relationships.

Each client that I have worked with is unique and has their own individual journey – it is important for me to ensure each client feels at the centre of their own journey and receives the validation they deserve as well as having someone to sit with them, throughout their peaks and troughs, to get to a greater understanding of who they are and move forward with their life with positivity and a full heart.

You are worthy. You mean something. It is okay to not be okay. You do not need to continue the self-sabotage. You do not have to be compliant. You CAN find who YOU are – or who YOU want to be. YOU can write your own life's story. It is yours.

Chapter 1: What, Who, Why, How, When, Where of a narcissist

In *'Why I wrote this book'* – I mention that narcissists leave more questions than answers for the person impacted by their presence or who is discarded from their orbit.

So, let's look at what or who a narcissist is.

Narcissistic Personality Disorder (NPD) is a serious disorder, and it has specific criteria to receive this diagnosis, and this can only be given by a mental health professional. A personality disorder, such as Narcissism, is a term that is given to someone whose thought patterns, emotions, and behaviour cause longstanding problems. A person must meet all three of the below criteria to receive this diagnosis:

- A person's thoughts, feelings, and behaviours cause you or others significant problems in daily life.
- A person's thoughts, feelings, and behaviours cause significant problems across all aspects of daily life.
- The problems continue for a long period of time.

So, the narcissist may be unable to trust others and have feelings of abandonment, for example, which in turn can cause unhappiness for the person or those around them. Creating and maintaining healthy relationships or friendships will be a struggle, as the person will not be able to control their emotions and behaviour in a home or work environment. These certain thoughts, feelings, and behaviours may have started in early childhood or adolescence and continued into adulthood.

A narcissist truly believes that they are special, and because they are special, it makes them different, better, and more deserving or entitled to anything and everything more than anybody else they are around. They have fragile self-esteem and are deeply insecure, which makes them reliant on others. This reliance is not exactly emotional dependence, but a reliance on others to recognise their own worth and needs. They can be easily annoyed if they are dismissed by others or if someone does not give them what they expect. They also reject and resent other people's successes, as these undermine the narcissist's importance. A narcissist will only put their needs first as other needs are not a priority, and will ensure that others put their demands as their priority as well. Others may see them as selfish and 'up themselves' or 'better than you,' and this is normally the case, as they have high expectations of others to increase and improve their status. In their journey to improve their status, they take advantage of others along the way and do not care about the consequences for each and every person that lays in their path.

Why?

Who knows what causes a narcissist? Many researchers think it is a complex matrix that does not come out with a significant enough reason. Could it be nature versus nurture? Or a mix of both? There could be a genetic factor, the environment they grew up in, or even childhood or adolescent experiences.

Genetics are involved in shaping our personality, as we are shaped by the people we are around from birth. At a certain age, we are then shaped further by our peers, environment, religion, politics, and society. Also, each baby has a different temperament, needs and wants. The reaction of a caregiver can affect a child's personality positively or negatively. (See the section - Adult of a narcissistic parent for attachment styles explanation).

When we look at environmental factors, a person is more likely to become a narcissist if they have had a chaotic or unstable home, which could include a parent having a mental health disorder themselves or addiction. Due to this instability, they could have had an unsupportive parent when they were navigating their emotional growth. This could be magnified if the child experienced a traumatic event and received no support at the time to heal their emotional void. This could also include a lack of support in an educational setting, with peers, or within their community.

Certain experiences that can affect a person in later life could be neglect by others, a sudden loss or bereavement of someone close to them, or a parent. They also could have been subjected to sexual, physical, or verbal abuse or even been involved (or witnessed) in a major incident or accident.

These experiences cement certain beliefs in the child or adolescent about how others think and how relationships should work as they get older. A child would implement coping strategies for themselves to move forward as a defence mechanism, and as they grow, these defences get stronger and distorted, which then are not helpful or healthy when utilised in adult life.

These unhealthy displayed traits of a narcissist could include:·

– *Grandiosity.* The person exhibits an inflated sense of self-importance and superiority. They are better than you – full stop.
– *Need for admiration.* They crave constant attention and admiration from others. This is fuel to them and creates their source of energy.
– *Lack of empathy.* They show no empathy towards other people's feelings and needs.
– *Sense of entitlement.* They believe they are entitled to special treatment and obedience from others. This is a need from them, not perhaps it may happen.
– *Exploitative behaviour.* They take advantage of others to achieve their own ends, without feeling

guilt or any remorse. They do not consider the consequences of their actions and do not care how they will affect others.

- *Envious of others.* They often envy others and believe that everyone is envious of them. These feelings of envy mean that someone else is receiving approval, and then they feel the attention is removed from them and will act out until the focus is back on them.

- *Arrogant behaviour.* They display arrogant, haughty behaviour or attitudes toward others. They must assert their power over others, and this is very important to them.

How, When, and Where.

The different stages of a narcissist are important to delve into to see how they work in and through a relationship with others.

There are three main stages with a fourth added on at the end, and these show what stage you may be in, in a relationship with a narcissist, or where you have been to feel validated in your process.

Stage One – The beginning – *Love Bombing.*

This is also known as the Idealisation stage. This is when you first meet the narcissist and they shower the object (you) of their affection with attention and admiration, in turn creating an 'ideal' and 'perfect' bond between you both. An almost too good-to-be-true relationship for you. They are creating their fantasy relationship with you, and they are putting you on a pedestal. They think you are the one that is going to fulfil the fantasy relationship they deserve and you are their new source of supply that gives them the energy and admiration that they demand.

Stage Two – The middle – *Devaluation.*

This could take months or even many years to get to this stage, but the narcissist begins to criticise you and devalue you as a person. This erodes your self-esteem and creates a co-dependency on them for their love and affection to be returned to you.

Ever heard of the term energy vampires? This is the term given to a narcissist, as they can completely exhaust you. They thrive on your wins, but also from your falls. The wins make them look important and enable them to be seen as having the perfect relationship. This praise and adoration give them so much energy to keep up their lies and manipulation. When you do something they deem as wrong or not good enough for them, they also gain energy in the way of being able to assert their control and power over you as being unworthy of them to create the addictive cycle of your need for them.

Stage Three – The end – *Discarding.*

This is where the narcissist ends the relationship with you, and this could be abruptly like it came out of nowhere for you. They withdraw their affection from you, leaving you confused and terribly hurt. You grieve for the person and the relationship and will try to win their affection back. Unfortunately, they have usually found a new source of supply (partner) to fulfil their fantasy relationship (which does not exist).

Stage Four – The 'just in case' – *Hoovering.*

Once you have been discarded by the narcissist, they may attempt to bring you back into their life with promises of change through their usual pattern of manipulation, continuing the cycle. This is usually the case when they are unsure whether their new source of supply will work out for them. This normally ends with Stage Three on repeat. This can be so devastating to the person who falls victim to stages three and four. Stage Three becomes final when the new source of supply ignites their energy enough for a new heightened fantasy relationship, which will allow them to be seen as superior once again. And they have this new source hooked on them.

Chapter 2: Child of a Narcissistic Parent

Looking back at your childhood, you may feel confused and unable to explain it properly to others. Your early caregiver (Mum/Dad or another person) displayed signs of love and dismissal quite seamlessly as early as you can remember. Questions you may have asked yourself are:

- Did you only receive praise when you had over-achieved?
- Was this praise often directed at others and not given to you?
- Were you dismissed when you spoke?
- Were you afraid of the consequences of having your own voice?
- Did you find yourself fighting fires to make them happy with you?
- Have you looked back and wanted to achieve or over-achieve to see them smile?
- People-pleaser?

You may have only seen that your narcissistic parent was different from others when you started to go to your friends' houses. The confusion was real. Was your parent a normal parent, or were your friends' parents wearing masks that you know your parent wears when around other people? You see everything through a different lens, of their adoration of you that was shown or discussed with others, but a lack of love and empathy at home. You just want to make them happy with you all the time, but it is a thankless task that, as a child, is frustrating and emotionally draining.

As a child, we want to be able to grow in a secure environment of love and support yet with challenges and boundaries to allow us to grow. The narcissist does not allow this safe, secure environment for their child. A narcissistic parent only shows you conditional love and for the child, this is a light in a long tunnel in achieving this – and the tunnel always seems to get longer and more distant at the flip of a coin.

To grow, a child needs to be able to use their voice and learn right from wrong in a positive and consistent environment. A narcissistic caregiver only reinforces how much you are a pain, a waste of time, not worth it, not valued or worth their time. Therefore, when you use your voice, it can be completely ignored (as if you had not spoken at all), spoken over, ridiculed, or shouted at to make you stop talking.

Over time, this lack of:

- Support
- Love
- Nurture
- Healthy Boundaries
- Empathy

- Room to grow

Gives the child not only frustration but also a lack of identity, self-esteem, and self-worth. The child becomes introverted, quiet, compliant, and anxious in and out of the home.

A child may attempt to rebel to get their parent's attention, but the consequences would be quite significant to the emotional well-being of the child. The parent would not want others to think they have failed as a parent. A rebellious child would cause others to talk about their child and their capabilities as a parent. A narcissist only wants to project a perfect persona of themselves and their family to the outside world. The consequences can range from anger, abuse, silent treatment, or removing the child from themselves in disgust. This then feeds into the child's view of self and that they have, yet again, failed to get the love, attention, and support that they crave so deeply from their caregiver.

As an outsider, a person only views you as a child as lovely, sweet, well-mannered, and a perfect child. They compliment the caregiver in raising a beautiful child who will go far in life. They do not see the emotional and perhaps physical scars that you have been subjected to daily. The threats that are made to you to ensure you are compliant, whether they are followed through or not, are deemed as real to the child as breathing. They live in fear of their parent being upset with them, as the anger can escalate so much that it is pointless for them to answer or fight back.

A child of a narcissistic parent is dominated in every aspect of their life. Everything they do is to ensure they are achieving and exceeding to make the parent happy with them – in the hope that they get a simple "well done" or "you did great today". Unfortunately, these are few and far between or even do not get vocalised to the child at all.

A child can think:

- Why me?
- What did I just do wrong?
- Why did they have me?
- I must be a horrible person.
- How can I make it better?
- If I do............. It may make them happy.
- When will I hear they love me?
- I just need to take my punishment and try better tomorrow.
- ·I just need to grow up and leave home, and then they may 'see' me.

Another confusing aspect for a child can be when they have sibling(s), whether younger or older.

If a child gets told that they are getting a new brother or sister, this could be quite anxiety-provoking for that child. They crave their parent's love, and yet, they are getting a child who could take their limited love away or even replace them and be the subject of more conditional attention.

If the child is not the oldest, they can have thoughts of needing to be more compliant to get more of their caregiver's attention. This could make them become an over-achiever, do more household chores (at an early age), and ensure their parent does not direct their anger or frustration at them but at another sibling instead.

Being a sibling of a narcissist allows the parent to hold greater control over you all. They can make you and your siblings compete against each other for their entertainment, to feed their manipulation and control over you. It could be that:

- Your brother/sister did better than you
- Try harder. Your brother/sister did it easily!
- Are you stupid? Your brother/sister did not need help from me.
- Why can you not be better at…... (Sport / Reading/writing / Musical instruments / Languages)
- I do not know why I had you.
- What is the point of YOU?

A narcissistic caregiver only wants to be perceived as the best person and the best parent – always better than other people, and their children are better children than those of others they meet. They expect you to live up to their sky-high, unattainable expectations. This allows them the opportunity to brag about you with their friends, family, or colleagues. It ensures that their high expectations are maintained, and the goals get increasingly higher with no reward for the child. Not exceeding your parents' expectations is not an option. They must ensure you are the best and better than other children. They could enrol you in many in-school and after-school activities to have a greater opportunity to brag. This may be exhausting for the child, but failure or asking to stop a club is not an option – unless it is the parent's idea. Removing a club will always be the child's fault, even if it was a financial decision for the parent. It will result in the caregiver making you feel worthless, unappreciative, and pathetic for them to have made this decision. This degradation, unfortunately, allows the narcissist to gain energy from this by asserting their control and power over their child.

When a child becomes an adolescent, the rush of hormones and a controlling narcissistic parent makes for a silently enthusiastic over-achieving teen or the opposite: a loud, argumentative rebellious teen that fuels the parent's need for even more control and power.

The strong, silent type still has maintained control, manipulation, and emotional, or perhaps physical abuse, but they understand they need to stay on the parents' good side and that one day they will receive the love and care they need from them – they just need to keep waiting. Hope is a keyword so that one day they will feel loved.

The rebellious, uncontrollable teenager is seeking attention and someone to hold and love them. This is not going to happen. It just increases the physical and emotional abuse, and the rules and negative boundaries are set stricter and harsher than before. This only results in two endings. The child becomes compliant again and lives in constant recrimination from that parent for not toeing the line, or the opposite - home becomes untenable, and the teenager gets thrown out of the home like trash (validating they are worthless and unloved) or the teenager leaves with no idea how to survive or where to go. The latter is very challenging for a teenager, as they have not been given the life skills to form and maintain healthy relationships with others. They only know how to be controlled and manipulated.

If a teenager leaves home - of their own accord later in life or earlier by the parent - this creates a dependency on others. A person from a narcissistic parent craves love and attention that they did not receive at home from one or both caregivers, and they will try to find it in any way they can. This can lead to the person involving themselves in risky behaviour or even seeking a narcissistic partner for themselves - as, unfortunately, this is the only relationship that they know.

Chapter 3: Adult of a Narcissistic Parent

So, attachment! Attachment by your early caregivers is one of the main theories of Psychodynamic counselling. It shows how you are as an adult in how you form emotional bonds and relationships by how you were treated by your main caregiver(s) as a child. There are four attachment styles, and I will describe each of them for you.

SECURE – this is the mecca! This is where we all want to be and expect everyone to have had as a child. The secure child experiences a healthy relationship with their parent and they can show an appropriate amount of distress when they are left alone. The child can seek support in their relationship with their parent and others and can regulate their emotions and manage conflict in close relationships.

AMBIVALENT – This shows that the child had limited availability of their parent and became distressed when left alone. An ambivalent child craves close relationships with others but then struggles to trust, so needs reassurance from others. The child also experiences feelings of anxiety and jealousy towards others.

AVOIDANT – Unfortunately, the child is subjected to abuse and/or neglect from their caregiver and they display no preference as to whether their parent is there or not. The child is seen as independent, but you can see an obvious pattern of withdrawal from them. The child will minimise the feelings of others around them as well as their peers and will not want to form close maintained relationships.

DISORGANISED – This is where a child has had inconsistent parenting and so, it leaves the child finding emotional relationships with others confusing. The child feels worthless and can project their frustrations in aggression or even unacceptable behaviour.

Which one do you identify with as a child? Now replace the word 'child' with the word 'adult.'

How does that feel?

Children of narcissistic parents mainly find themselves having a disorganised attachment.

All is not lost, with therapy – talking to the right professional, you can heal and move through the attachment styles to get to a secure attachment. It CAN be done, and it happens all the time.

Identifying your style – allows you to see where you need to be or even if you see it in others – you can help them and support them along the way. Knowledge is power and understanding gives direction and purpose.

So, what age were you when you found out your parent was a narcissist? As an adult, you would have always known that your upbringing was different but do not know any real difference – other than seeing your friends, colleagues, or partners' parents and wondering if everyone wears a mask in front of other people. The realisation comes, it always does. It can be a slow burn or a tornado ripping through your heart.

When you come to the realisation, you can feel lost, confused, frustrated – even grief. The 'aha' moment does not necessarily come when your parent dies – it can come knocking when they are still alive, and you feel immense guilt at feeling these confusing emotions surrounding your parent.

Did or do you ever ask yourself:

– Were you or are you a people pleaser?
– Whatever you did was not enough?
– You class yourself as an over-achiever.
– You never have enough hours in the day – but still prioritise your caregiver.
– You still love them – so much. So, why does it hurt?
– One day they will say they are proud of you.
– One day they will say they love you – and mean it.

- How did you not see it before?
- Why could you not have a 'normal' parent?
- Why could I not be a child and have a normal childhood?

The last question you ask yourself starts the loss and grief process – and this is a very real emotion. You start to grieve for the parent who may still be here, or not, for not being a normal parent able to give you a normal childhood. This can be quite painful and emotional, and so many questions start to spin around you. Why did this happen to me? Could my parent be fixed? Will I be like them? How do I stop the cycle?

A narcissist very rarely can change. They may seek help when they are pushed to it if they feel they will lose something they value. It is a long and slow process – as a narcissistic person cannot show empathy and anything negative that occurs is not their fault – it is yours.

Your parent needs your energy to thrive – so the attention they crave may make it impossible to maintain a healthy relationship with others. The guilt and embarrassment of your caregiver's needs create distances between other relationships, that the parent enjoys the demise of. It allows them to gain greater satisfaction from being in control and deepens their manipulation of you as well as our desire to please and placate them.

Accepting your caregiver for who they are is a task. The energy you provide to them is never going to be enough. It can create so much tension within you that it affects your health, well-being, family, and work relationships. The disorganised parenting style you received may display itself in you as causing these internal conflicts in finding, maintaining, and loving your relationships with others.

One of the main questions I get asked by clients when navigating the maze that is their parents, is 'Am I a narcissist?' – answer: No! A narcissist does not have empathy or regard for other people's feelings. Therefore, a narcissist would never consider this question of themselves. An adult, of a narcissistic parent, also worries they will affect their children with their parent's traits. Just identifying your early caregiver as a narcissist allows you to not implement or follow your caregiver's parenting style and be mindful and nurturing of your child(ren)'s relationships with that grandparent. This is a great shift for you, as you will be able to move forward with clarity in your life.

Another question I am asked about is 'Do I need to stop seeing my parent?'. That choice is yours and yours alone. You can, absolutely, continue to see your early caregiver! You may need help and support in your emotions, thoughts, and behaviours, and in doing this, you can find your inner strength, to set clear and strict boundaries for yourself when dealing with or being around that parent. This is to help and support your health and well-being and move forward with a healthier and brighter outlook.

Others may find a need to stop contact with that parent altogether. This is a personal and individual choice. They may need to access talking therapy to navigate their loss of childhood, loss of a parent, and loss of a huge chapter of their life. Again, prioritising yourself is paramount to you living the life you want to, free from any chains or links to the past that you can work through.

If your narcissist parent has died, it is important to navigate your confusing grief – again, of a lost childhood, a restrained adult, potentially, and the parent you had always wanted to appear. This grief journey can be long and arduous, but coming to terms and accepting that person could not change for you will be instrumental to your healing journey.

Always seek help by talking to friends and family or a professional. Talking helps you find connections and make sense of your memories and reality. This allows you the headspace to start breathing and realise you are enough. You deserve love.

Chapter 4: A Friend or Family Member of a Narcissistic Person

These relationships can be quite strained and appear difficult to navigate from a family member's or a friend's point of view with a narcissist. They may even no longer be a friend or associate themselves with the family (or you with them) due to their behaviour.

In a relationship or friendship with others, a narcissist is a pathological liar who creates a false persona to show the world how fantastic they are and of their wealth, achievements, experience, and status. This, unfortunately for the narcissist and those around them, is all built on lies. The trouble is that the narcissist believes their lies, therefore they do not think they are saying anything that is not true about themselves.

The narcissistic person can be very dismissive of your achievements. So, in a family situation, if a family member achieves a status higher than them, they will dismiss this achievement as something lower down the scale, to ensure they stay at the top of the family tree to be admired and respected. In a friendship or a friendship group, this will also be the case, that someone else cannot possibly be better or achieve greater things than the narcissist. In playing their games of 'I am the best', they may make mistakes or do something that others do not like (to ensure their status remains) but will be completely dismissive of their wrongdoings – as nothing is their fault. Someone else is always to blame for the situation, or someone else created the drama that they are not a part of – therefore remaining critical of others. The manipulation of the situation and others is prevalent, as you believe what they are saying;

therefore, you believe that someone else or something else created this negative occurrence.

They will constantly seek to control you and the situation to remain powerful – whether this is the small family unit or the wider friendship groups. This control is very important to them and creates a sense of calm for them as they are directing the ship of their lies and manipulation.

In their presence, they are charismatic and will boast and exaggerate their life, their wins, and their importance to gain praise and admiration from you, as this provides them with much-needed energy to continue their path of manipulation and lies in getting to where they need to be.

A narcissistic person also likes to make false promises to make you feel important to them, but it will only leave you feeling disappointed. Even though it may have happened time and time again, you are left still feeling so happy with their promises when they are made, only to feel disappointment and rejection when they do not happen for you. You may think 'not again', but the narcissist knows how, when, and what (love, gifts, etc.) to entice you back to them.

Narcissism and addiction can be co-conspirators. The narcissist does not allow people to say no to them, and they think they deserve whatever they want – whenever they want it. No matter the consequences of their actions, they are like a spoiled child whose parent gives them sweets to placate them, so they do not make a scene in public. This excessive need gives way to over-indulgence in whatever field they find themselves dancing in. This can be alcohol, drugs, gambling, sex, or more. Even though you may see it as an outsider and question their behaviour, they will not think there is anything wrong with it and potentially try to involve you in their risky behaviour ultimately to then blame you if anything goes wrong.

All the above culminates in the narcissist showing you that they are two-faced. They can change from Jekyll to Hyde quite quickly, sometimes without skipping a beat, depending on how you react to them.

Narcissistic rage is a term that is very much real. If they think you are 'on to them' and their attempts at blaming you for their mistakes are not working, they can become very easily irritated, which can turn into sudden outbursts. These outbursts can be quite shocking and even scary. When you are subjected to the narcissist's rage, you become dismissive and apologetic to calm the narcissist down – as you know it is your fault (as they tell you it is!). It is not your fault, and when you realise this, the relationship with your family member or friend can get very strained. You start to see through their lies and start to question your relationship with them.

This can lead to irreparable damage to your relationship with them, which is when the narcissist becomes on the periphery of the family and group. This enrages the narcissist, as they are powerful and in control of everything and everyone – so it is better for them to gas-light others and remove themselves from the situation, leaving a trail of blame and disgust directed at you. You are left feeling very confused about what happened and who the person exactly was to you. You do feel great sadness that they are no longer part of the group or family, as you get to see what hurt they caused and the tension that was felt when they were around.

The charming and charismatic narcissist knows how to wear their mask well. They are master manipulators who make themselves look attractive in every sense of their life. Then the mask slips.

Chapter 5: A Partner of a Narcissist

A narcissist creates a fantasy of the intimate relationship they will have with their partner, one that makes them powerful and admired. They choose you because you have something that will feed them by giving them their much-needed energy through importance, whether it is beauty, fame, power, knowledge, status, or money. You will become their 'source of supply.'

The 'source of supply' is a term used to describe where the narcissist gets their energy from. The adoration creates strength for them, and in seeing this, they decide you are theirs. This is where the love-bombing comes from. They shower you with gifts, holidays, praise, and adoration, and you can truly think, 'This is too good to be true'. Your friends and family see how you have 'landed on your feet' by getting someone who adores you as much as they do and who treats you like a king or queen. This is where the narcissist is at their best. They have managed to manipulate you and others into their fantasy world of sunshine and rainbows. You do not see the wood for the trees for quite some time.

You love that you are adored and that your family and friends love them just as much as you do. You feel happy that your future is going to be amazing with your newfound amazing love.

Your new love must create a version of themselves that they think and believe they are. This is based on fiction and a bed of lies, but their charisma, charm, and manipulation draw you in until you are addicted to them and your relationship.

The narcissist will never want anyone to know about their lies and wrongdoings, so they will assert their control over you. This is to keep up the happy mask and perfect life persona to everyone else as perfect. But you may start to question what they may have said to you and how that differs from what they say or have said to others.

You will not see a different side to your partner for some time, perhaps even years or decades. Looking back on this point in your relationship can be hard for you to acknowledge.

The stage after being love-bombed is devaluing, and this can start very subtly that you will not even know when it started to happen. You are made to adore this person, so anything that goes wrong or does not happen for them – is your fault. So, you try to constantly make things better by fighting fires and by always trying to calm the situation down, placate them, or be one step ahead of their mood swings and outbursts. This can create anxiety and low mood for you. But you get no sympathy or empathy from your partner – as it is not conducive to their well-being. They do not want what you want, and your perceived negativity feeds their self-importance. The criticism of you becomes intensified as you can 'never do anything right' or they make personal attacks on your appearance. This feeds their ego as they feel, again, in control of the situation and you. This constant reacting, surviving, and muting yourself to attempt to make the narcissist happy is exhausting and can be frightening at times. Ultimately, your sense of self and your self-esteem becomes zero.

The fantasy relationship that the narcissist created in their head starts to wane, and they make sure you know it is your fault – but it is not. No one can live up to the extremely high unattainable image they have in their heads of what a relationship should and must look like.

They may even suggest that it is a sexual reason that you are not attractive to them anymore and suggest different sexual acts or vices that they may like to try – and by participating in these, you are showing them you love them still and that you are trying to please them by whatever means they suggest. Unfortunately, you may not want to do these intimate sexual things and be disgusted at yourself for trying them – in a last-ditch attempt to make them love you like they did before.

But as they have full control over you, you are unable to see this and want to keep making them happy. The love-bombing is a distant memory for them, but for you, you crave this from them again and think if you can just do one more thing, they will adore you once again. This one more thing becomes several until you lose count – but you keep trying and fighting for their love and kindness.

During the devaluing stage, a narcissistic partner has normally found a new source of supply for their energy to be revitalised once more. They have started to see a new opportunity at the unattainable fantasy and have decided that you are not part of it and that a new source of supply is the right decision for them. They may suddenly not return home, abruptly leave, or even be dismissive of you and find pleasure in you pleading for them to stay.

This rocks your world, your future, and your love for them. You are left confused, alone, and not knowing which way is up. Due to the intense manipulation from the narcissist, this can manifest in Post-Traumatic Stress Disorder (PTSD) as the narcissist has made you who they wanted you to be – for them, through manipulation, and this has made you addicted to them. Addicted to the immense highs you had when you were in the love-bombing phase and the intense need to make them happy to gain their affection. So, without them, you have no idea what to do and are constantly thinking about how to get them back, only to be constantly dismissed. The pain you feel is so very intense, and each day can feel like forever and drain you of energy to keep fighting for their attention.

Unfortunately, as mentioned before, the 'hoovering' stage may come into play, which is constantly brutal to be a part of. When the narcissist finds a new source of supply, they may be unsure that the new person is perfect for them. So, what they do is constantly keep you dangling in their affections, as a 'just in case'. This gives you hope that they will return to you, that you are loved, and that your future is going to be okay with them in it. This is a blip, and they will realise you were made for them and all will be well.

The narcissist may continue to manipulate you, especially if you have decided to be strong and not go back to them, by saying things like:

  – You said you loved me?
  – You obviously never loved me in the first place.
  – Why won't you fight for us?
  – Why can't you see we belong together?

The love-bombing may even reappear in the way of gifts and attention.

This is to suck you back in, ready for them to spit you out if the new source of supply gets stronger, and then they move on without a sidewards glance back at you. This constant rollercoaster of emotion is crippling and confusing.

The addiction to this person cannot be understood by someone who has not experienced a narcissistic attachment to someone. The questions that follow from your friends and family can feel so intense when all you want to do is find out what you did wrong for the narcissist and make it better.

The next chapter discusses what an ex of a narcissist looks and feels like.

Chapter 6: An Ex of a Narcissist

Harsh words, but they no longer care for you. You are no longer giving them the life that feeds an unrealistic fantasy they expect for themselves to gain constant adoration from others. This abandonment hits you heavily and hard.

The term 'trauma bonding' applies in the case of a narcissistic relationship. It is where the narcissist has manipulated you and the control is so intense that it creates an abuser/rescuer situation. You basically fall in love with your abuser, so when they start to treat you badly in the discarding stage, you crave their past attention and think that somehow, with your help, they will change, and it will be back in the love-bombing stage, and you will be able to make them happy again. This is the addiction – an addiction to the narcissist, which leaves you constantly dangling, waiting for them to be in a good mood or happy with you.

This can be devastating to come to terms with not only for you but especially if there are children involved. The children are also discarded, and this is a double stab to the heart, as you must navigate your grief and loss as well as the hearts of your children.

A narcissist may use your children as a constant source of fuel to keep you in the 'hoovering' stage. This may only be to ensure the children are over-achieving to enable him to brag about them and keep his friends and family thinking his life is utterly amazing and what a fantastic parent he is. In the meantime, they may cut contact with the children or want the children 100% or 50/50 to assert their power and control over you. This is always about them and never anything about you.

They leave you with no energy to fight and no finances to

attempt to. By this stage, they have normally had full control over the finances throughout your relationship, and they think you are not worthy of having financial independence from them – or even deserving of maintenance if you have children.

If you have had a 'light bulb' moment and realised you have been living with a narcissistic partner and you have mustered the strength to leave of your own accord, this is amazing. But you already know the battle in front of you. They will ensure everyone thinks that you are the problem without leaving you alone. The barrage of calls and texts knocking at the door can be intense. This is to try and make you 'give in' and go back to them. This causes the narcissist shame and embarrassment, and they will feel anger and even rage towards you. Always remember your own safety at this point. Reach out to your family and friends for support or even professional organisations. Your health and well-being are important to move forward safely away from the narcissist.

If, by their choice or your own, the relationship is no longer serving its purpose, they may make you feel like even if you tried to go up against them, you would be making a fool of yourself, that they would win anyway – and to roll over and play nice like a 'dog.' This may be with friends, family, a solicitor, the family court, or finances. They have no interest in you as a person, as an ex, or as a parent of their children.

This allows the devastation to manifest within you. You feel shame and guilt that no one would understand. You still cannot understand what you did wrong to make them leave you or treat you this way, and ultimately, they still have control over your thoughts, feelings, and behaviours.

You may have already been subjected by friends and family to:

- 'Don't be silly - they are amazing.'

- 'How great they were for you.'

- 'What did you do?'

- 'How did you let this happen?'

- 'How could you have changed to keep them?'

- 'If they love you, they will come back?'

- 'You could have tried harder?'

- 'You need to let them see their children.'

- 'Would the children be better living with them until you're sorted?'

- 'Pull yourself together. No wonder it did not work out.'

- 'You just need to go around and apologise to them.'

And perhaps many more. None of which are helpful or constructive to you when you already think it is all your fault. The charm and charisma that radiate from them ensure the manipulation continues and that no blame lies at their door. Only yours. The power struggle is non-existent - you have no energy left.

Ensuring you talk to others or seeking professional help is important for you now. Talking therapy, with whoever, allows you a safe, confidential space to talk about your life, talk about your relationship, and talk to someone that creates a space for you to be open and honest and make connections between what is true and the lies.

It is your time to grieve for what could never have been - and this can be so very distressing but also, in the end, empowering.

You were not at fault. You were not to blame, and you are worthy.

You now need to look at how to grow after your pain and restore your sense of self and belonging.

This may be a hard and long journey of self-discovery. There may be pain and tears - but there is also a chance for healing, seeing the world in full colour, and making beautiful, happy memories moving forward for you.

Chapter 7: A Survivor of a Narcissist

Strange to read this? Yes, you can and will survive your narcissistic relationship. It won't be easy, and it can be a hard road of highs and lows – but there is a path forward for you.

Regaining your sense of self and what makes you happy is the most important part to become a brighter you and attain a brighter future without manipulation.

Coming to terms with the stages of a narcissist, learning about their traits and how they behave can create a sense of calm in the end. It was NEVER your fault. You became a victim of a narcissist who used you for their own gains. This does not mean you are worthless. This means you are worthy. It was just manipulated for a period of your life when you were not allowed to see the wood for the trees. You do not have to account for your every move anymore. You do not have to walk on eggshells not knowing what could cause an outburst next. You do not have to be fearful of his actions. You do not have to listen to them blaming friends, family, or colleagues for their actions and placate them that they are amazing and will get something even better than what they wanted.

It may take time for your friends and family to realise the actual life you lived. But they will. A common statement from a client's friends that I hear in therapy is 'I am so sorry, I feel I have failed you'. They did not fail you as a family member or a friend – it just means that the manipulation from the narcissist worked. It was not just you who experienced it. You cannot ask for help when you are made to think it was you all the time.

Now is the time to progress the four attachment styles mentioned previously into Love and attachment styles. You can read this when thinking of the narcissist, or where you are now as the present you.

Secure love and attachment – again, the mecca that we all strive for. The signs you are in this style are:

- 'You have a positive and stable sense of yourself.'
- 'You have a positive and stable sense of others.'
- 'You are interdependent (not dependent or independent).'
- 'You are comfortable with intimacy.'
- 'You are open and trusting.'
- 'You see yourself as an equal with your partner.'
- 'You tend to stay connected when you are apart from your partner.'
- 'You can set and respect boundaries.'
- 'You rely on yourself and others to manage any distress.'
- 'You welcome diverse perspectives.'
- 'You seek connection but also can provide space.'

Anxious love and attachment style is also known as the 'Pursuer' (can be seen in the attachment style as Ambivalent):

- 'You have a negative and insecure view of yourself.'
- 'You have a positive and stable view of others.'
- 'You tend to be dependent.'
- 'You fear losing your relationship.'
- 'You have emotional ups and downs.'
- 'You elevate your partner above yourself.'
- 'You tend to be clingy when apart.'
- 'You are worried about being disappointed or being abandoned.'
- 'You are anxious but with diverse perspectives.'
- 'You tend to be the pursuer in this relationship.'

The Avoidant (Withdrawer) attachment and love style would show the following:

- 'You have a positive, yet unstable view of yourself.
- 'You are negatively insecure in your view of self and others.'
- 'You are independent and self-reliant.'
- 'You fear intimacy.'
- 'You elevate yourself above your partner.'
- 'You show reluctance in relying on others.'
- 'You view dependency as a sign of weakness in others.'
- 'You have set rigid boundaries (erected walls as a defence).'
- 'You can challenge diverse perspectives.'
- 'You seek distance and avoid attachment.'
- 'You withdraw and avoid any conflict.'
- The last is the Fearful (Disorganised) love and attachment style:

- 'You have a negative and insecure view of yourself.'
- 'You have a negative and insecure view of others.'
- 'You seek yet avoid closeness.'
- 'You long for love but reject intimacy.'
- 'You struggle with scorekeeping (in arguments).'
- 'You fluctuate between being expressive and supportive to distant and unavailable.'
- 'You can set boundaries but then do not maintain or respect them.'
- 'You embrace yet reject diverse perspectives.'
- 'You pursue love but withdraw to avoid being hurt.'

Whichever one you think you fall mostly in, everyone is striving for a secure attachment. This is not unattainable, whatever your hurt or pain. Use this as a source of information to see where you are at NOW and then where you want to be.

Your life is now yours again. Your children (if you have them) have their own lives too. You will be able to get strong enough to navigate their relationship with their other parent – in time. In your time. The shift of power to equality can be slow and exhausting at times. But know that there is always another survivor cheering you on. You are part of a tribe, and you are not alone. A tribe you did not ask to be a part of – but an amazing tribe all the same.

What are your next steps?

Where will your own shoes and your own heart take you?

Your life's options are limitless – not limited. Take time to heal and then fly.

Chapter 8: Coping Strategies with or without the Narcissistic Relationship

We all develop coping strategies from birth to allow us to protect ourselves in whatever situation we find ourselves in – whether this is physically or emotionally.

Some coping strategies create healthy defences for us to maintain our health and well-being. Other coping strategies are defences we use at the time as we may be unable to help or protect ourselves. These can distort our narrative but then manifest into unhealthy coping strategies moving forward.

When we are in or out of a narcissistic relationship, the narcissist thrives on manipulation and control over us. This can, as mentioned, create a negative self-image and lower your self-esteem. This can create an anxious and nervous persona as you are always on guard, waiting for the narcissist's disapproval or rage.

If you have read in previous chapters about your attachment and love style, we all want to move towards a secure attachment style. This creates a sense of self-worth and a positive outlook and therefore a brighter future.

To be at the centre of your own journey is important, even if you are staying in your relationship with the narcissist – as ultimately, the narcissist should put you in the centre of your relationship, as that is where love blossoms and thrives.

To move forward, where you can be at the centre of your journey, there are some healthy coping strategies that you can try to understand yourself and to maintain your positivity.

Self-compassion. Being compassionate to yourself may feel foreign at first – but you had it before – it is just about finding it again and moving forward to find yourself. It is important to replace your inner critic, the voice that tells you that whatever you do is not good enough. We all have an inner critic, but yours may have become more powerful by being fed by the narcissist. Journalling can be a great tool to use for this. To be able to write down your negative thoughts, feelings, behaviours, and that of others can be very cathartic. You are getting all your negativity out of your head and 'handing' it to someone else. 'Handing' is writing it down and 'someone' is your journal. Some people like to keep their journals to reflect on. This validates your thoughts and negative things that have happened that day. It allows you to plot your journey, appreciate the highs, and understand the lows. Some people like to write everything down and then destroy it – like it has gone from their mind and now gone from their space. The decision is yours – the journal and experience are yours. Yoga and mindfulness are other great ways of being compassionate to oneself. Connecting with your body and learning and practicing breathing techniques allow you to be present as well as being able to self-regulate negative emotions and stressful situations. There are many different types of yoga, whether these are accessed online or in-person, just try a few and see what you get the most enjoyment out of. As with mindfulness, there are also paid-for and free apps online that you can use at any time during the day. You can start with a few minutes and increase to longer as and when you need to. Mindfulness is something to be practiced until you understand it and get benefit from it. Some people like silence, some like a type of music, and others like guided where a person instructs you through the journey. Find what works for you and do not put pressure on yourself. You will get thoughts when meditating or practicing mindfulness, and that is OK. It is the thoughts, connections, and peace we can find within and afterwards.

Be outside. Sounds simple, and some days it may feel like a task or chore. Being outside, even if it is for a minute outside your back door or a long arduous journey up a mountain – the choice is yours. Being able to observe the birds, or just listening to them with your eyes shut – or even the silence around you can diminish anxiety and enhance our mood. This, in turn, allows us to find clarity in our thoughts, feelings, and behaviours.

Be creative. Do not think you are creative? Does it matter? You used to be creative, but do not have time or fell out of love with it? Then you can be creative in finding what you like! Whether it is music, drawing, painting, scribbling, pottery, baking, cooking, photography, or more – you can express so much emotion when creating your own art. You may not be creating a Picasso, but it is yours, and whatever it turns out as – you created it and should be proud of yourself for allowing yourself the time to dedicate to yourself and your process of growth. You may even want to find a class, to be with others in a social setting in creating something. Or prefer to be alone to immerse yourself in this cathartic experience. Find what works for you.

Move. Movement is good for our body and mind. Did you used to have a favourite that you would like to re-engage in, or would you like to try something new to see if it makes you happy? This can be a gentle walk, a dance class, cycling, attending a gym, or booking onto a class. See if a friend or an old friend would like to go with you, and then you are not only helping your mind and body, but you are also being social and engaging with others, creating a greater support system for you.

An important one is in *setting boundaries* for yourself and others - healthy boundaries. Boundaries can be for anything – how someone talks to you, how they treat you, and how they make you feel. Knowing what you want in the present and the future is important – as this can guide you in thinking, creating, and maintaining your boundaries. Maintaining boundaries with a narcissist can be quite daunting and hard to maintain, but sticking to these is important for you and important for the narcissist, as it allows them to know when they have overstepped your boundaries and to understand why and allow them to apologise if the situation calls for it. In maintaining your boundaries, you are validating yourself and acknowledging your importance and worth.

You can also *organise* your home and work life. In finding yourself, you can find what you like and what you want in your surroundings. This allows you to find and create your 'vibe' in the two places you spend most of your time. This ultimately creates pleasure and accomplishment when you have the idea and see it come to fruition. This also allows you to find self-regulation, as you may find some aspects hard – but you continue and see the positivity in your actions and that fulfilment at the end. You may even get appreciation from others in creating your 'vibe' or even gratitude and positive affirmations. Understanding your positive compass allows the positive self-talk to speak over your inner critic – which can only be a good thing.

On your journey to self-discovery and healing after pain, *self-care* is very important for you. Ensuring you find what makes you happy is important in knowing which direction you want to take yourself in. Concentrate on what makes you happy, and regularly 'check in' with yourself to monitor how you are doing.

Forgive yourself. You are not to blame for where you were or where you are now. You can rediscover the world around you, and each step may take strength. You used this strength before to survive – now you can use your strength to thrive.

The narcissist created the narrative that you had no choice but to adhere to.

Now, it's time for you to write the rest.

Chapter 9: How to Help a Narcissist

A narcissist must recognise their behaviour is different from others and their behaviour has a negative effect on themselves, their loved ones, and those around them. This can be a long journey – or even one with no end, unfortunately.

If the narcissist accepts their thoughts, feelings, and behaviours are negatively impacting their lives and those of others, there are a few things that they can do – or you can help them access.

- They will need to speak to their GP to be referred to a mental health professional for a diagnosis (Psychiatrist).
- There is stigma around getting a diagnosis for some, but others find receiving a diagnosis helpful in explaining why they have their thoughts, feelings, and behaviours.
- Talking therapy. This can be with a counsellor, who specialises in narcissism. This is not a short-term therapy and may be a long journey for the person when entering therapy.
- Support groups. An individual may find it better for them to join a group to support each other in their journeys to understanding and change.
- Medication. This is not for narcissism but could be helpful if the person suffers from depression, anxiety, or something else. This can be discussed with their GP or mental health professional.
- Being involved in their journey. Ensuring that the narcissist develops good relationships with their medical or health professionals is important to how they move through their journey. This allows them to feel they have a voice and can successfully move forward through what may be a hard maze to navigate for them.
- Take charge of their well-being. A narcissist needs to find something that makes a significant difference to how they feel. This could be:

    o Talking to others. Sometimes, it can be hard for them to reach out and have difficult conversations with loved ones or friends – but this will be helpful for them.

o If they ever find themselves in crisis – to know who to reach out to – either their GP, 999, or their local NHS Crisis team.
o Peer support. They may find they prefer face-to-face support groups, whereas others may like online support groups – whichever they choose would be helpful to enable them to find connections with others with understanding and without judgment.
o Coping strategies. If they feel their behaviour has a trigger, they should find something that they like, which will create a healthy way to think, feel, or behave. This could be from journaling, meditation, drawing or painting, exercise, certain music, or smell – something to 'ground' the person to make them feel in the here and now and not in an unhealthy past situation.
o Sleep. Ensure they have a good sleep pattern, as this allows them to have the energy to cope with the day ahead.
o Food. Creating a healthy diet helps to give their bodies the right nutrients and energy to cope when they are finding things difficult.

What can you do to help a narcissist?

A narcissist finds creating and maintaining their relationships hard to navigate and can make them feel anxious about looking at their relationships with others. You have probably always found it hard to say the right thing when you are with them, as their behaviour toward you may have been unpleasant in the past.

Patience is important, as they may be struggling with their emotions. If an argument starts to occur, just wait for calm before talking things through with them. This can be hard at the beginning, as they will think you are shunning them. Therefore, always talk to them calmly and with compassion as you know they are trying to change their thoughts, feelings, and behaviours – but they are having an internal battle between what they want (a healthy outcome) and what they think they deserve (an unhealthy usual outcome). Listening to a narcissist allows them to feel validated in their emotions and acknowledged by you, but by honouring your boundaries and expectations. These expectations and boundaries for your relationship must be agreed upon by both of you and strictly adhered to by both parties to ensure that you move together towards a healthy relationship and future. This also allows the narcissist to recognise when they have done something unacceptable to you and your relationship. It also allows them the time to reflect, consider you, and apologise if needed.

An important aspect is to look after yourself. Living with or around a narcissist can be extremely upsetting and you may never know what is going to happen – keeping you on edge. Ensure that looking after your own mental health and wellbeing is paramount. Talk, listen, and seek your own support. If you are not fit and healthy in all senses, you will not have the energy for yourself – let alone the person you want to help through this.

You need to:

- Seek help, support, and talk to others.
- Make and maintain healthy relationships with others (whether this is with or without the narcissist in your life).
- Set healthy, strict boundaries for yourself and the narcissist (if you are in a relationship with them).

- Safeguard your self-esteem – their thoughts, feelings, and behaviours are a reflection on them, NOT you.
- Stay calm. Listen. Then start a healthy conversation, ensuring you can say how you feel and maintain your importance as an equal.
- Recognise your worth.
- Take time for yourself to know who you are, what your goals are, and how you want your future to look.
- Your present and future have endless possibilities. What are yours?

Chapter 10: What a Healthy Relationship Looks Like

Understanding your own wants and needs in a relationship is very important. We are all unique, and our individual life experiences and future goals are not the same as others – so finding your butterfly moment and then building a strong foundation for a successful long-term relationship can be extremely different from what your friends or family may or may not want for yourself. For example, one person may find in their tick list of wants that their future partner's looks and humour rank highly to have a fun and engaging relationship, yet another person looks for wealth in their own life and that of their partner, which is highly attractive to provide security and a comfortable lifestyle.

You also must remember that high expectations in your tick list must be flexible. Ideal partners never tick all the boxes! It is like buying a house or a new car – there is always something you must prioritise over certain things to ensure that you are going to get your 'ideal' person. Another way to look at it as well is – are you perfect? Unfortunately, none of us are, however we try to be. We all have strengths and weaknesses, and knowing what these are and understanding them allows you to seek help in your relationship as and when you need it. Can you put up a shelf, but are unable to cook a risotto – but your partner cannot do DIY, but is a great cook? Compromises are key, as are some boundaries.

We all need boundaries in all aspects of our lives, whether it's with a friend, parent, family member, child, partner, or work colleague. Healthy boundaries are fixed and put you and your health and well-being at the centre. Such things could be:

- I will not allow someone to break my trust.

- I will not allow someone to abuse me – verbally, physically, or emotionally.

- I want a supportive, engaged partner who is on the same page as me.

- I have my beliefs and values, and I need someone to have the same.

Flexible boundaries could be:

- I want a partner who has a well-paid job position.

- I would like a partner who takes the bins out.

- I want a partner who does not rate intimacy highly.

- I do not want to get married.

- Children are not a part of my future.

Healthy and flexible boundaries are yours and yours alone. They can move positions or remain fixed – depending on how highly you rate them. But understanding your boundaries and accepting that some may change is a great way to start your relationship journey.

If you are currently in a relationship and did not or do not have clear boundaries – that is fine! There is never a barrier to open and honest conversations in your relationship, so starting a conversation with your partner over joint values and beliefs allows you to get closer and open a dialogue for change or a deeper understanding of each other.

When you know your personal beliefs and values and what is important to you as an individual, and as a couple – then you can start to see what type of relationship would be good for you.

It may seem like an obvious exercise, but we will look at what an unhealthy relationship looks like first. This may be helpful as signs to look out for, or for friends and family to take note of any signs of in a friend's or family member's relationships to help someone move towards a healthier relationship (with or without their current partner).

A negative, unhealthy relationship can and does normally start off as the unicorns and rainbows phase that is often called the 'honeymoon' phase, and we wear 'rose-tinted glasses.' This is where we fall in love and find out more about our partner and lay the foundations for a relationship. When the 'honeymoon' phase ends or the rose-tinted glasses come off, you may not see that you have entered an unhealthy relationship due to manipulation and control. This can start off very subtly, and you may see the red flags, but you do not recognise them until much later or not at all.

A controlling and domineering partner will try to alienate your friends and family, to the point that these interactions get less and less and possibly stop altogether. They start to tell you what to wear and that they prefer you to stay with them rather than go out socialising without them. They have great charm and charisma with your friends and family, showing an outside persona as something very different when you are together. The mind games start where they become critical of you, your actions, your thoughts, and your appearance to lower your self-esteem and assert more control over you. This control allows the manipulation and lies to manifest. They will deny that they are at fault or that a negative comment or experience has happened, or even that an abusive moment occurred or its significance. There is always something else they blame their actions on also – whether this is drink, drugs, stress, work, or you! When things do not go their way, they express themselves towards you with a 'look', get angry, shout loudly, hit or break things, or even go childlike with sulking or not speaking to you.

If they think that you will leave them, or potentially speak out and tell someone what is happening or ask for advice, they will cry and say they love you, or even that they will kill themselves, leaving you feeling guilty and to blame if they did. They threaten you, or even your children, with harm or to kill them to make you stay with them. They may even threaten you with reporting you for abusing them or your children or any government services if you are in receipt of benefits – to assert their control over you. You must remember that your partner is King (whatever the identifying gender), and that you are merely their slave and servant, to do their bidding. They will expect a clean home, dinner on the table, financial control, and sex on demand. Having sex with them is a command and not a question, and this can get to extremes of them forcing you (raping you) for their satisfaction, as NO is not in their vocabulary. They may even repeatedly demand children from you (if in a heterosexual relationship) to keep you pregnant, to stop others from wanting you, and to stop you from leaving them. On the flip side of this, if your partner does not want intimacy with you, they will constantly reject you but make you feel that something is wrong with you as to why they do not want any intimacy or sexual relationship with you.

If you do have children, they will always think that they are the better parent and put you down about your parenting style. They will ensure they talk bad about you in front of the children and manipulate them to think that you are, in fact, a bad parent in their eyes. If you are no longer together, they will use the children as pawns to gain access to you and to threaten you that they will get the children away from you. They may even make you have a baby with them, so you are a family unit – and then reject you and the baby and refuse to help or be a part of that child's life. This all adds to their idea of how important they are and how you must bow down to their demands, as your life is theirs and you are no longer able to have your own thoughts and feelings without checking with them first.

Does this sound like a power imbalance? There should always be equality in your relationship to ensure you are both having your needs met while ensuring you are looking after your health and wellbeing. Looking inward and maintaining a healthy sense of self and future automatically allows you to think of others and spread your love and kindness. Stifling your sense of self disables your positive and happy outlook.

So, you know what you do not want for a friend, a family member, your child, and therefore yourself.

Are you unsure what a healthy relationship looks like? You may not have had perfect role models to instil in you what is acceptable or unacceptable, and this is fine. Staying true to yourself, your wants, and desires are your building blocks for a bright future.

What should you be looking for in a partner, that maintains equality, love, and trust? This person is not too good to be true – their actions are decent and pure. They make time for you to listen and talk to you as a friend and a companion in life. They have a similar sense of humour to you and a positive outlook. A partner will be able to show you affection and gratitude without expecting sex or intimacy and takes no for an answer from you. They will take your intimacy seriously and be able to gauge if you do want sex and be involved in making decisions that affect both of you regarding contraception or what your sex life will look like. They will love your sense of family and embrace them as well as your friends, seeing them as an extension of you and your support system. They will encourage and support your life outside of your relationship, whether this is socialising, hobbies, or taking time out for self-care (trips away etc). They will want to support you in your dreams and goals in your career and pick you up if you stumble, and be the emotional crutch and sidekick on your journey to be who you want to be in your career. They will show you how much you mean to them not only in the occasional gift – but more importantly in words. They will say they love you, you look good, and that they had a great time with you (even if you are in a long-term relationship and living together!) They will value you as a person and your opinions on things – even if you agree to disagree on certain subjects. A partner will help you nurture your strengths and help with weaknesses as they know you are competent at whatever you choose to do as they value your commitment to yourself, your life, and your relationship with them. In turn, they can be responsible for their own well-being and happiness and behave like a responsible adult with you (but also know when you can be silly and fun together too!). In accepting responsibility for their actions, they can apologise when they need to or accept blame without blaming something or someone else. Your partner will help with the house, with finances, and treat you with respect and equality.

If you are parents, you can be a responsible influence in the children's lives. They do not get the children to favour themselves over you and are active in being an equal parent in their emotional, physical, and financial future.

Does this sound amazing?

Now do you do this, or will you do this in return? That is equality in a relationship – you can expect it, and you should, but you also must be able to be that person for your partner too.

Share both of your values, beliefs, and aspirations.

Always promote open and honest communication.

Listen and don't instantly react to each other. Everyone has a right to an opinion and to be heard.

Repairing a relationship is doable – you just both need to want it, work at it, and rekindle your spark.

Show kindness and compassion to yourself and each other.

Relationships should always be nurtured, however far you are into your journey.

Passion is great – but so is empathy, compassion, trust, loyalty, and so much more.

Love yourself to be able to love someone else.

Reach out for help and support when you need to.

You've got this.

Useful contacts

BACP - British Association for Counselling and Psychotherapy

www.bacp.co.uk for a list of counsellors near you.

Elefriends

www.elefriends.org.uk is a Friendly, online, supportive community for anyone experiencing mental health problems.

Emergence

www.emergenceplus.org.uk is a Service user-led organisation that supports people affected by a personality disorder for – service users, carers, family, and friends.

(NAPAC) - The National Association for People Abused in Childhood

0808 801 0331 www.napac.org.uk is a Charity supporting adult survivors of childhood abuse.

NHS Choices

www.nhs.uk Provides information on personality disorders as well as your local crisis teams.

Mind

0300 123 3393 www.mind.org.uk The National Association for Mental Health provides information on diagnoses, treatments, and practical help. Mental health legislation and where to get help.

If you or someone you know is in crisis – do not hesitate to contact your GP, 999 or local NHS Crisis Team.

www.ingramcontent.com/pod-product-compliance
Lightning Source LLC
Chambersburg PA
CBHW070939120626
46546CB00004B/1473